Krazy Kool
Kinetic SAND!

Are you ready to explore the fun world of kinetic sand? All you need is some basic tools, some special sand, and your imagination to get started! Kinetic sand is moldable toy sand made with 98% real sand that you can mold, cut, shape, stamp, and more without needing to sit in a sandbox or on the beach! Because kinetic sand sticks to itself, it's easy and clean to work with. It feels super gooey and fun but without any of the mess! Explore the ideas in this book to see what you can do with some of this very special sand, and enjoy!

You can make all the projects in this book with regular or colored kinetic sand!

Let's Explore Kinetic Sand

Let's Create with Kinetic Sand

16

A Day at the Beach

18

Medieval Sand Castle

20

Great Pyramids of Egypt

22

Tropical Volcano

24

Sunken Treasure

26

Construction Zone

All About Kinetic Sand
Ask the Kids!

> Kinetic sand is way cooler than regular sand! It stays molded, it moves and flows, it feels good, and it doesn't stick to you. You can't resist it—you just have to touch it.

> Kinetic sand is like wet sand that flows and doesn't stick to you or anything else. It looks like sand, but when you touch it, it reminds you of play dough or brown sugar.

> If I had 1 million tons of kinetic sand, I'd make a giant sandcastle... or a giant cat... or a life-size building I could go inside!

It Oozes, Melts, and Flows!

This sand almost seems to come alive! It is dynamic, kinetic, and organic. As it moves, it fascinates and enchants children and adults of all ages!

Lava Flow

Somewhat gently, pack sand into a tall, narrow cylinder. Turn the cylinder over onto a flat surface. Slowly pull the cylinder up to remove it from the sand, and watch the column of sand flow down and out like hot, oozing lava. Try leaving the cylinder on the top half of the sand while the bottom oozes for a minute. Try several cylinders of different sizes and widths and see which flows best. And try packing the sand really tightly or not packing the sand much at all.

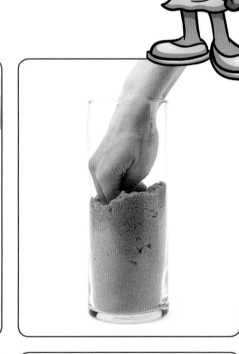
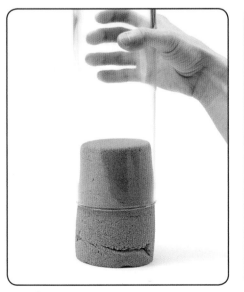

Hourglass Fingers

Create an hourglass effect with your own fingers and watch the way sand flows quickly. Hold two fingers of one hand as shown in the photo, forming a circle. Lift up a big pile of sand with the other hand and set it on top of your hand forming the circle. Some of the sand will fall off the top of your hand, and some will flow down through the hole. See how it slides and separates in little chunks and tendrils. Wait until the sand has stopped falling, then do it again, this time making a larger circle (without your fingers touching). The sand flows in very interesting ways.

It Rolls, Stamps, and Prints!

Kinetic sand compresses beautifully! It's almost therapeutic to roll and smooth this sand into a flat canvas. It is absolutely amazing how it takes such beautiful, crisp, and detailed impressions! Within minutes, curiosity will spur on creativity and give way to many fun printing experiments. To try the following ideas, first use a brayer, rolling pin, or glass jar to roll out a smooth, packed flat sand canvas.

Custom Roller

Use hot glue to write, draw, or create designs on a smooth, cylindrical glass jar or vase. Roll the cylinder over the sand canvas to reveal the custom print. Once you are finished with the designs that you have created with the glue, you can simply peel the glue off the glass and create a new design! Hint: In order to read the messages, be sure to write backwards. You can check your work by looking through the other side of the jar to read the message before you print.

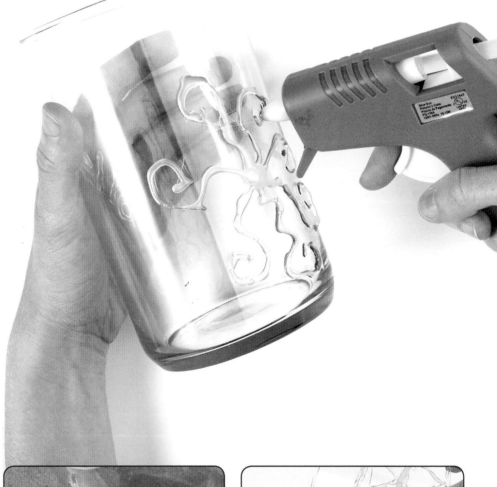

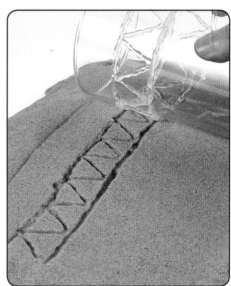

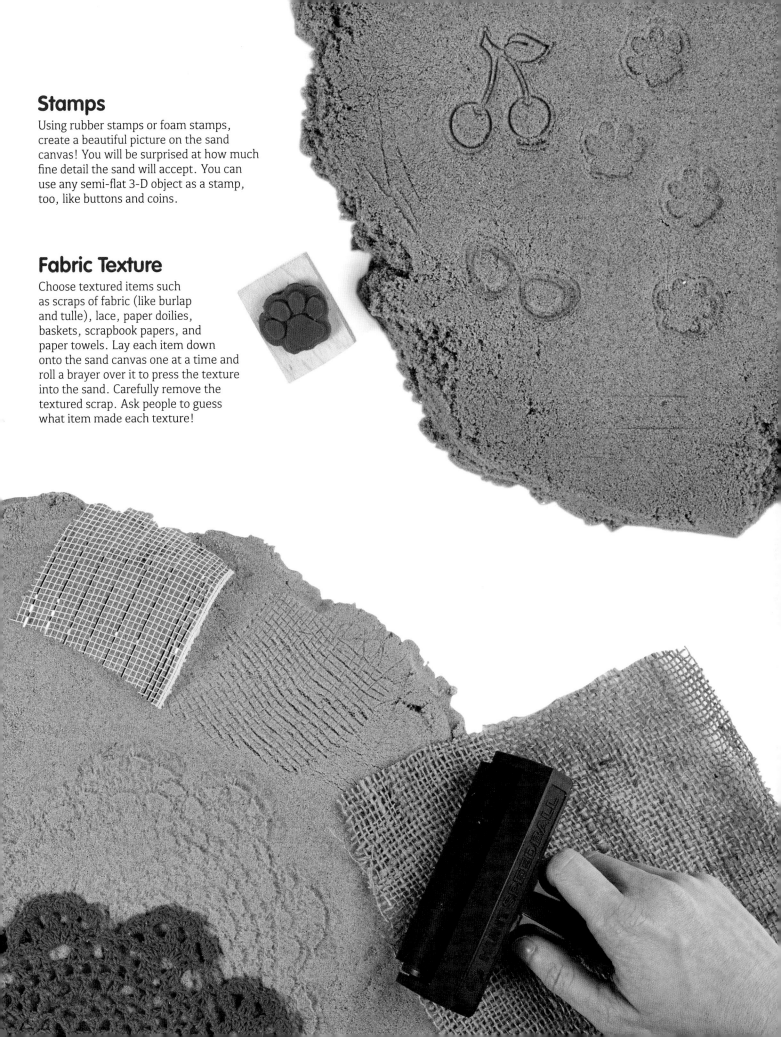

Stamps

Using rubber stamps or foam stamps, create a beautiful picture on the sand canvas! You will be surprised at how much fine detail the sand will accept. You can use any semi-flat 3-D object as a stamp, too, like buttons and coins.

Fabric Texture

Choose textured items such as scraps of fabric (like burlap and tulle), lace, paper doilies, baskets, scrapbook papers, and paper towels. Lay each item down onto the sand canvas one at a time and roll a brayer over it to press the texture into the sand. Carefully remove the textured scrap. Ask people to guess what item made each texture!

Kinetic Sand Superpower: Super Shapeshifter!

It Forms, Molds, and Slices!

This amazing sand packs into so many different molds and retains the fine detail of each! You can turn sand into almost any shape you can imagine! Beyond molding, you can take a fine straight-edge and enjoy slicing and dicing sand into small, crisp pieces. Cutting the sand is surprisingly mesmerizing and fun!

Basic Steps for Molds

1. Fluff. With your hands, fluff up the sand until it's light and airy.

2. Ooze. Fill the mold, allowing the fluffed sand to flow into all the crevices.

3. Pack. Tamp the sand down evenly with your hands or using another object such as a smooth jar or box bottom.

4. Scrape. Remove any excess sand from the top of the mold using your hands and a straight-edge cutting tool. Make sure that the tamped sand is level in the mold and doesn't dip down below the mold edges.

5. Flip. Turn the mold over onto a flat surface. For very large molds, it may be best to turn the flat surface onto the back of the mold first, and then turn them both over together.

6. Clean. Slowly remove the mold from the sand; depending on the shape of the mold and how well you packed it, you may have to tap it to get the sand to come out. Use a straight-edge cutting tool to clean up any stray sand and smooth over any cracks.

Letter Cutting

Using the rectangular solid template mold, follow the molding steps to mold a 3-D rectangle. Then slice the rectangle into even pieces. Form letters with the pieces to spell words. Smooth the connections between the pieces with your fingers. See what other interesting shapes can be molded and sliced! There are many ideas suggested in this book.

1. Pack the sand. Pack sand into a rectangular solid template mold and shave off any extra on top.

2. Clean the rectangle. Release the rectangle and make sure the edges are nice and clean.

3. Cut slices. Cut slices of the rectangle with a straight-edge cutting tool to make pieces for shaping letters.

Tips for Cutting

* Always use a long, straight edge that is longer than the cut you need to make. A relatively sharp metal spatula works well. But try to find an edge that is all one thickness, not one that tapers to a point—most table knives taper, though they will still work fine.

* Line up the cut and then apply fast, even pressure—don't be slow and don't linger.

* Start cutting in the middle of the sand object and work toward the right. Then go back to the middle and work toward the left. This will evenly distribute the spacing between the cuts and keep the piece centered in the workspace.

Experiment with Kinetic Sand

Tube Ooze

Cut 1", 3", and 5" (2, 7, and 12cm) long toilet paper roll or paper towel cardboard tubes. Pack sand into the tubes while holding the tubes upright on a flat surface, then remove the molds by sliding them off from the top. How does each cylinder of sand move and ooze? Do they stay upright or fall over? Be patient and watch the three columns. What conclusions can you make about the way kinetic sand works?

which Will Fall First?

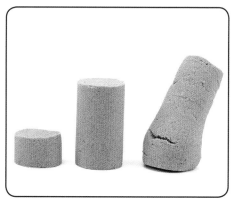

Time Lapse Snowman

Form one small ball about the size of a golf ball, one medium ball, and one large ball. Draw a face on the snowman's head with a toothpick if you like! Quickly assemble the snowman. With a stopwatch, record the length of time it takes for the snowman to melt. Do the individual balls melt slower or faster than one another? If you make a smaller or larger snowman, what happens? What are some ways you can pack the snowballs for a slower melt?

oh No, I'm Melting!

Build and Destroy

See how strong and high you can build a brick wall. Experiment with different brick shapes and wall designs. Start with the small and large brick template molds, ice cube tray blocks, or bricks cut out of a larger square mold. How high can you build the wall? Do smaller or larger bricks melt the slowest? Do molded or cut bricks melt the slowest? What is the best pattern of bricks to place for the most secure wall? Build the catapult shown on page 18 and use it to destroy the wall you built!

Staggered big bricks. This wall uses the big brick mold and an alternating pattern.

Columns of big bricks. This wall uses big bricks simply stacked up.

Staggered small bricks. This wall uses the smaller brick mold and an alternating pattern.

Columns of chopped bricks. This wall uses bricks cut from one big molded rectangular solid.

Experiment. You can use many different brick shapes and sizes to build a wall.

Creative Tools to Use

There are so many things to do with kinetic sand—the possibilities are endless! Interacting with just the sand itself will provide hours of fun, but once your creative juices start flowing, you will want to have some of these tools on hand. A lot of them are already in your home, and special items can be found at your local craft store.

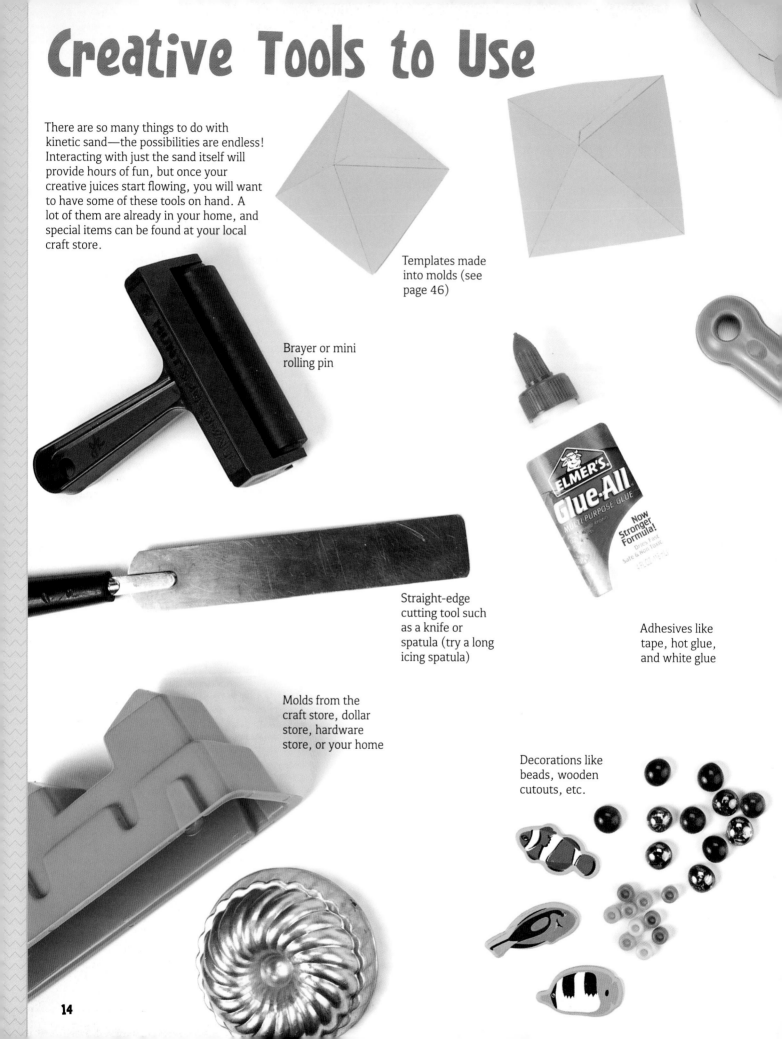

Templates made into molds (see page 46)

Brayer or mini rolling pin

Straight-edge cutting tool such as a knife or spatula (try a long icing spatula)

Adhesives like tape, hot glue, and white glue

Molds from the craft store, dollar store, hardware store, or your home

Decorations like beads, wooden cutouts, etc.

Kitchen items like measuring cups, bowls, and trays

Kitchen utensils like spoons, forks, spatulas, pizza cutters, ice cream scoops, and melon ballers

Stamps

Texture rollers

Scrapbook paper and foam for scenery and bases

Small toy figurines

Clay carving tools, toothpicks, and pencils

A Note About Bases

For each diorama-style project in this book, there is a suggested base used, but you can use whatever type of base you want! Try large pieces of foam, shallow trays, flower pot bases—whatever you can find that's fun and easy to play in! You can even paint a base to make it ocean blue or grass green to suit the setting.

Important Tip!

Kinetic sand is 98% sand. Work on a protected surface, or you will soon see scratches on the work surface, especially if it is made of wood!

A Day at the Beach

Create a perfect day on your favorite beach! If you could visit any beach in the world, which one would it be?

1. Create the setting. Choose a blue base like a shallow, circular blue pan. Use string to hang a wooden sun or a sun cut from yellow foam in the background, or tape the sun to a background.

2. Create the beach. Drop fluffy sand along the back half of the setting to create the sandy beach. You can pat it down a little if desired, but don't make it too packed or smooth.

3. Add the dunes. Make two denser piles of sand to one side of the beach for sand dunes. Smooth them down with your hands. Poke pieces of grass into the dunes.

4. Add accessories. Decorate the beach with toy figures like chairs, umbrellas, fencing, shells, or whatever you like.

5. Make the pier. Break three craft sticks into pieces about 2" (5cm) long to use as a base for the pier. Using hot glue, glue them on top of the other six craft sticks lying side by side. Be careful of splinters.

6. Add the pier. Add some sand sticking out from the front of the beach. Place one end of the pier on the sand so that it sticks out from the beach into the water.

Ideas:

* Stamp footprints in the sand with a footprint stamp.

* Write messages in the sand using a toothpick.

* Build a mini sandcastle using a tiny ¾" (2cm) diameter flowerpot as a mold for turrets.

Materials:

▌ **Blue base**

▌ **Wooden sun or yellow foam circle**

▌ **Fresh, dried, or fake grass**

▌ **Toy beach figures (chairs, umbrella, fence, etc.)**

▌ **9 craft sticks**

Did you know?

There are more than 17,500 lighthouses in the world speckled over 2,000,000 miles (3,218,688km) of the world's coastline and painted in different colors and designs so sailors can easily recognize them during the day.

Medieval Sand Castle

Design a mighty sand castle that demonstrates your wealth and strength in medieval Europe! Guard it with knights, and build a catapult to lay siege upon the walls until they fall!

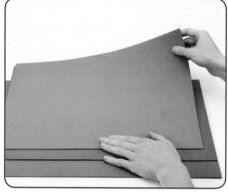

1. Create the setting. Lay down a large sheet of green foam for grassy land, then lay down a large sheet of blue foam on top of it as shown. Cut down a smaller sheet of green foam and lay it on top of the blue to form a moat on three sides.

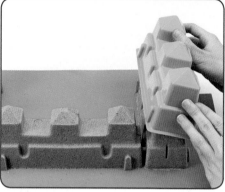

2. Build the castle. Use real sand castle molds to build an impressive sand castle of three or four walls. Make sure to pack the sand firmly into the molds to make the castle strong!

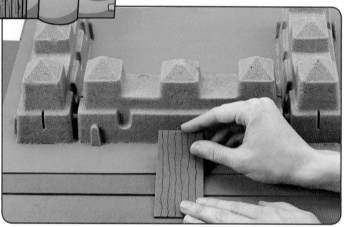

3. Create the drawbridge. Cut a rectangular drawbridge from gray foam and draw plank lines on it with a black marker. Lay it in place over the moat, making sure it connects to the land on each side.

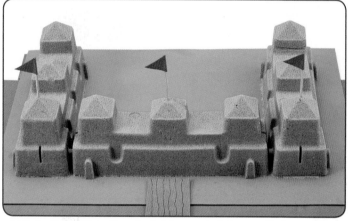

4. Make flags. Make flags by folding and gluing small pieces of red cardstock or paper around the tops of toothpicks. Place the flags in the turrets of the castle.

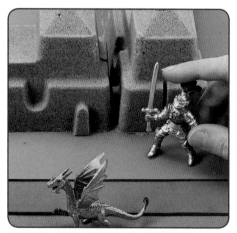

5. Add knights. Add toy knights to the scene to protect the castle. You can even add some threatening dragons for the knights to fight.

6. Lay siege. Build a catapult out of a plastic spoon and some craft sticks using hot glue. Load sand "rocks," real pebbles, or ping-ping balls into the catapult and fire them at the castle walls!

Ideas:

* If you are feeling ambitious, add little buildings inside your castle using the brick template molds.

* Model a castle after your favorite castle in history or literature—maybe even King Arthur's Camelot!

* Build two castles with a friend and have a battle where each of you catapults "rocks" at one another's walls until they all come tumbling down!

Materials:

- **4 sheets 12" x 18" (30 x 45cm) foam: 2 green, 1 blue, 1 gray**
- **Sand castle molds**
- **3–5 toothpicks**
- **1 sheet red cardstock or paper**
- **Toy knights, horses, and dragons**

Did you Know?

During the medieval period, the time between the fall of Rome in 476 CE and the fall of Constantinople in 1453, castles were built all over Europe. They were constructed with circular stairs climbing clockwise so that those at the top defending the castle would have the right-handed sword-fighting advantage.

Great Pyramids of Egypt

Create your own archeological expedition just outside Cairo on the banks of the Nile to discover the hidden secrets of the Great Pyramids and the giant Sphinx.

Did you Know?

The largest pyramid of Giza is called the Pyramid of Khufu and is 481' (146m) high and 756' (230m) long on each side. It contains more than 2 million blocks of stone that each weigh more than 2 tons (1,814kg)!

1. Create the setting. Set a wooden box lid against a wall and tape sky-colored paper on the wall behind it using painter's tape. Add a palm tree in one corner. Cut a Nile River from blue glitter paper and place it as shown.

2. Mold the pyramids. Using the pyramid molds, mold two or three pyramids and arrange them as shown to one side. Hide a treasure inside each pyramid!

3. Mold the Sphinx body. Fill the toilet paper roll cylinder mold with sand. Push it out gently to release the body onto the empty space beside the pyramids.

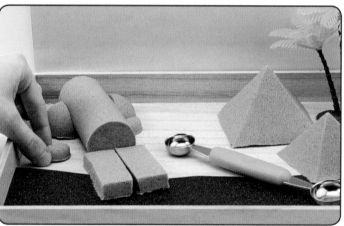

4. Mold the Sphinx legs. Cut two front legs from the rectangular solid mold. Mold a ball with a small cookie scoop, cut it in half, and place one half on each hip. Mold a ball with a melon baller, cut it in half, and place one half in front of each hip for back paws.

5. Mold the Sphinx head and tail. Use the cookie scoop to create a round shape, set it on its side, and press it down to make it a rounded semicircle. Gently press some sand to the front to make the noseless face, and set the head on the body. Add a long tail.

6. Add accessories and details. Place toy Ancient Egyptian figures near the pyramids to populate the landscape. Use clay carving tools or a pencil to add detail to the sphinx face and paws. Draw block lines on the pyramids to make them look realistic.

Ideas:

* Form an expedition with small human figurines and camels. Can you discover a new pyramid?

* Dig for the secret treasures hidden inside the pyramids. Can you find them all without destroying the pyramids?

* Roll out some sand and draw your name in Ancient Egyptian hieroglyphics.

Materials:

▌ Wooden box lid

▌ 2 sheets 12" x 12" (30 x 30cm) scrapbook paper: 1 sky color/pattern, 1 blue glitter

▌ Plastic palm tree

▌ Large, medium, and small pyramid template molds

▌ Small treasures (gems, coins, etc.)

▌ Toilet paper roll cylinder mold

▌ Rectangular solid template mold

▌ Toy Ancient Egyptian figures

Tropical Volcano

Seek out a faraway tropical land where the mountains are high and the trees are beautiful! But if you feel the earth rumble, get ready to run!

1. Create the setting. Cut a corner of fake grass sheet to fit in one corner of a green box lid. (Don't mix the sand with the fake grass, as the grass will shed small pieces that will get mixed in with the sand.)

2. Prepare the volcano. Pack sand into a glass vase, packing the bottom half tightly but the top half gently. You only need to pack about 7" (43cm). Turn it over onto the setting.

3. Create the volcano. Slowly raise the vase, leaving the top of the vase over the top half of the sand to keep it balanced for a bit as it flows and oozes to create the volcano. Then remove the vase. Gently press a crater in the top of the volcano.

4. Add greenery. Plant a fake bush, fern, or palm tree in one corner of the setting to make it tropical and lush.

5. Add flames and lava. Cut flames out of orange and yellow foam or tissue paper and place them in the volcano's crater. Cut orange, wavy strips of lava to overflow the crater and run down the side of the volcano.

Materials:

- Green box lid
- Fake grass sheet
- 3" (7.5cm) diameter by 12" (30cm) high cylindrical glass vase
- Fake bush, fern, or palm tree
- 2 sheets 8½" x 11" (21.5 x 28cm) foam and/or tissue paper: 1 yellow, 1 orange

Did you Know?

More than 75% of dormant and active volcanoes are found in the ring of fire, an area in and around the Pacific Ocean. There are two active volcanoes on the Hawaiian Islands, one of which has added hundreds of acres of land to Hawaii.

Ideas:

* Read *Treasure Island* by Robert Louis Stevenson, a classic tale of tropical treasure.

* Hide buried treasure at the base of the volcano in an additional mound of sand. Carefully make a treasure map so you can find the treasure again when you return.

Sunken Treasure

Explore this mysterious shipwreck at the bottom of the sea. Perhaps you will find a chest filled with gold and jewels!

1. Create the setting. Lay down turquoise foam for the ocean floor. Lay sand mixed with gems down in the middle.

2. Make the treasure chest. Mix gems into some sand and shape the sand into a treasure chest by cutting the cube mold in half and the toilet paper roll cylinder mold in half lengthwise, or molding it freehand.

3. Add coral. Set a piece of dried coral or a starfish down in the scene.

4. Sink the ship. Construct a few main pieces of the ship from a wooden ship kit, and then lay the partially constructed ship and some loose pieces, such as the mast, on the ocean floor.

5. Add accessories. Decorate the scene with wooden fish, a wooden pirate flag, and any other desired items.

Ideas:

* Send down a diver to explore the shipwreck.

* Find all the jewels that were lost in the shipwreck.

* Observe marine life, look for fossilized shell prints, and collect a few previously unknown specimens.

Materials:

- Container to hold sand
- Item for impression/candle shape
- Wick
- Pillar candle
- Wide-mouth glass jar
- Pot of simmering water
- Potholders or tongs

Did you Know?

Candles used to be used as clocks! Some candles were made to burn at a consistent rate and had regularly-spaced markings on them, which allowed for marking the passage of time.

Games

Each of these games is so much fun, and you can play them over and over again!

Coin Roll Race

1 or more players

Materials: a few coins

Directions: Build a sand mountain and carefully roll each coin down the mountain to create a grooved track for each coin. Then race the coins down the mountain. See which coin rolls the farthest, the fastest, or for the longest time. What kinds of extreme coin-rolling tracks can you create?

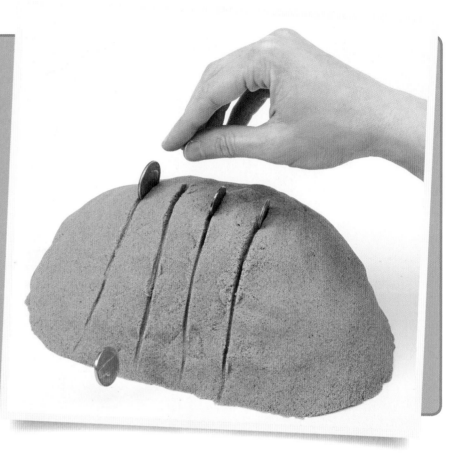

Pink

2 to 4 players

Materials: paper, pencil, pony beads: 10 orange, 8 blue, 4 yellow, 2 green, and 3 pink

Directions: All players mix and hide the pony beads in the sand. The first player to go digs out a bead. That player gets the number of points indicated by the color of the bead pulled. That player can continue to pull out beads and continue to add up points until they either decide to stop and keep the points they have won, or until they pull a pink bead. If a player pulls a pink bead, they lose all the points they have won during that turn and the next player begins their turn. Keep a running tally of the points that you have at the end of each turn. Return the beads to the sand once the 3 pink beads have been pulled. The first player to reach 50 points is the winner. Points are as follows: orange = 1 point, blue = 2 points, yellow = 3 points, green = 4 points, pink = you lose your points from the round.

Pig in a Pen
2 players

Materials: rectangular tray, brayer, pencil or skewer, 1 bead per square each in 2 colors

Directions: Use a brayer to flatten the sand in a rectangular tray. Use a pencil or skewer to make holes in a grid pattern across the sand playing board at least 11 holes high by 11 holes wide. During their turn, each player can draw lines between two dots at a time (but no diagonal lines). If you are the player to draw the final line that completes a square, write your initial or place a bead in your chosen color on that square. You also get to take another turn every time you close a square. The player at the end with the most completed squares is the winner!

What's Missing?
2 or more players

Materials: tray, 20 small items, sand mold large enough to hold each small item

Directions: Place 20 small items on a tray. Show the tray to the players for one minute. The first person to be the Hider takes the tray away and hides one item inside a sand mold. The Hider then places the molded sand in the center of the tray and takes the tray back to the players. See who can guess the item hidden in the middle of the mold first. You have to have a good memory! The winner of the round gets to be the next Hider. If all the players are stumped, then they can ask questions of the Hider which the Hider can only answer with a "yes" or "no."

Templates

Making Molds from Templates

Materials: paper and pencil or photocopies of templates, scissors, glue stick, cardboard (poster board or cereal boxes), masking tape

1. Copy or trace the outline of the mold you wish to make on paper.

2. Cut the mold out of the paper.

3. Glue the paper mold to the cardboard.

4. Cut the mold out of the cardboard.

5. Fold the mold on the fold lines. To get a clean and crisp fold, score the fold lines with the straight edge of a table knife.

6. Tape the sides together to make the 3-D shape of the mold.

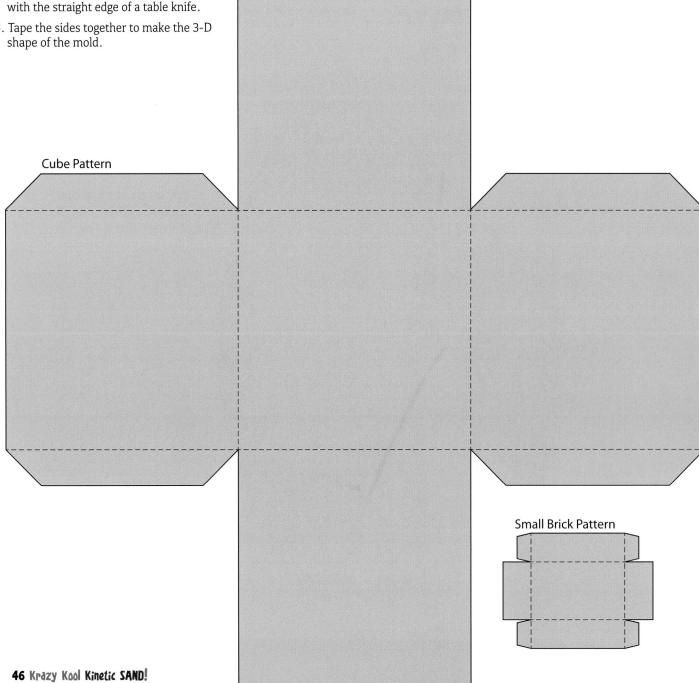

Large Brick Pattern

Cube Pattern

Small Brick Pattern

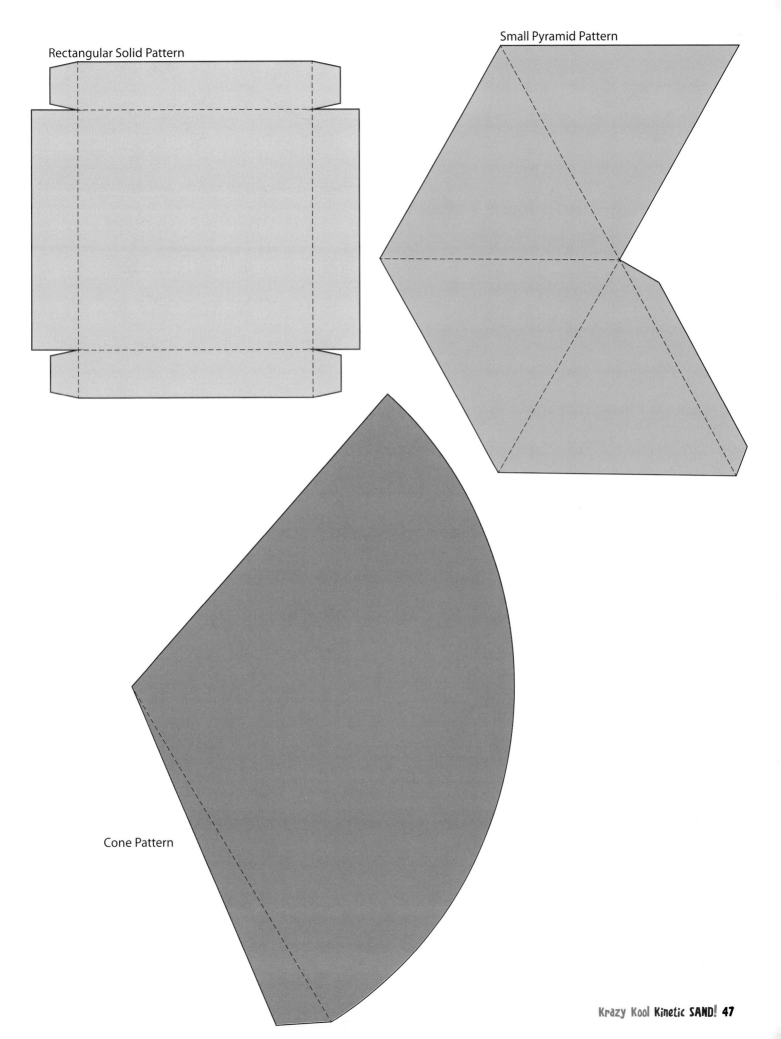

Rectangular Solid Pattern

Small Pyramid Pattern

Cone Pattern

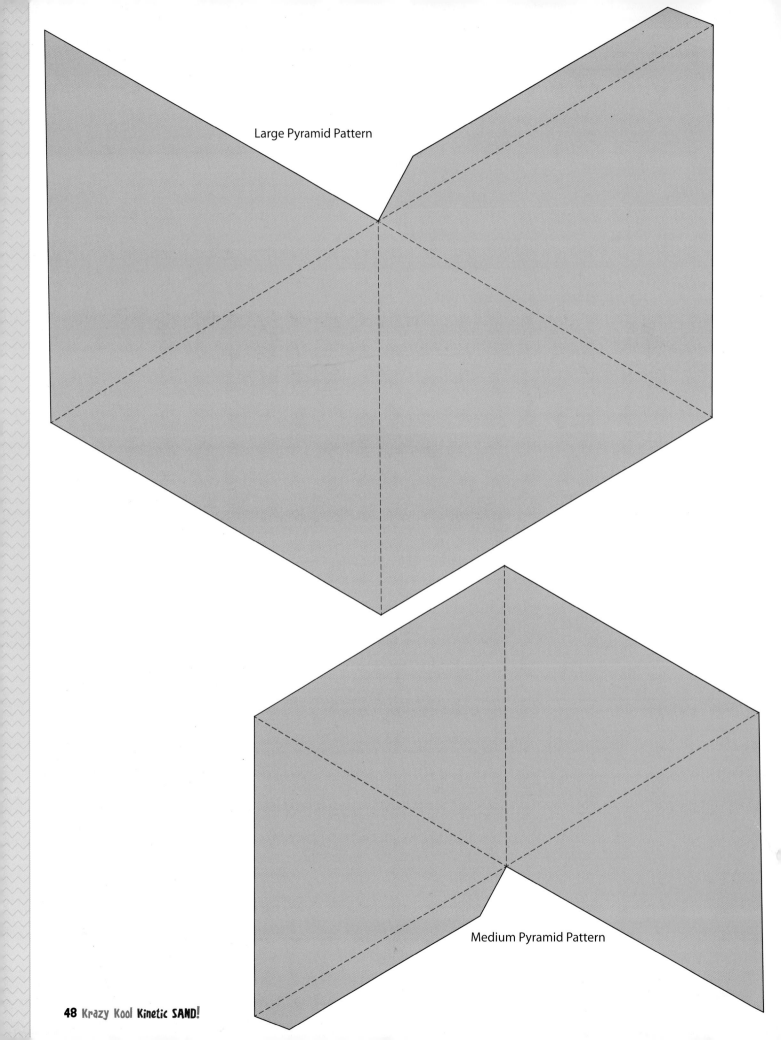

Large Pyramid Pattern

Medium Pyramid Pattern